D0510912

EARTHMOVERS

by Lee Sullivan Hill

Lerner Publications Company • Minneapolis

02782004 - ITEM

To my husband, Gary, with love. —L.S.H.

Text copyright © 2003 by Lee Sullivan Hill

All rights reserved. International copyright secured. No part of this book may be reproduced, stored in a retrieval system, or transmitted in any form or by any means—electronic, mechanical, photocopying, recording, or otherwise—without the prior written permission of Lerner Publications Company, except for the inclusion of brief quotations in an acknowledged review.

This book is available in two editions:
Library binding by Lerner Publications Company, a division of Lerner Publishing Group
Soft cover by First Avenue Editions, an imprint of Lerner Publishing Group
241 First Avenue North
Minneapolis, MN 55401 U.S.A.

Website address: www.lernerbooks.com

Library of Congress Cataloging-in-Publication Data

Hill, Lee Sullivan, 1958–
    Earthmovers / by Lee Sullivan Hill.
        p. cm. — (Pull ahead books)
    Includes index.
    Summary: Introduces the parts and functions of different kinds of earthmoving machinery.
    ISBN 0–8225–0689–0 (lib. bdg. : alk. paper)
    ISBN 0–8225–0603–3 (pbk. : alk. paper)
    1. Earthmoving machinery—Juvenile literature.
[1. Earthmoving machinery.] I. Title. II. Series.
TA725 .H54 2003
624.1'52—dc21   2001006139

Manufactured in the United States of America
1 2 3 4 5 6 — JR — 08 07 06 05 04 03

EAST SUSSEX

| V | BfS | INV No | 7458657 |

| SHELF MARK. | JY 629.22 |

| COPY No | 02782004 |

B R N

DATE | LOC | LOC | LOC | LOC | LOC | LC

COUNTY LIBRARY

Do you like to dig in the dirt?

Earthmovers dig tons of dirt. They dig sand, too. Dirt and sand are kinds of earth. Earthmovers are made to move earth.

They push earth.

They scoop earth.

They pack it down hard.

An **operator** makes an earthmover go.
An earthmover's operator sits in the cab.

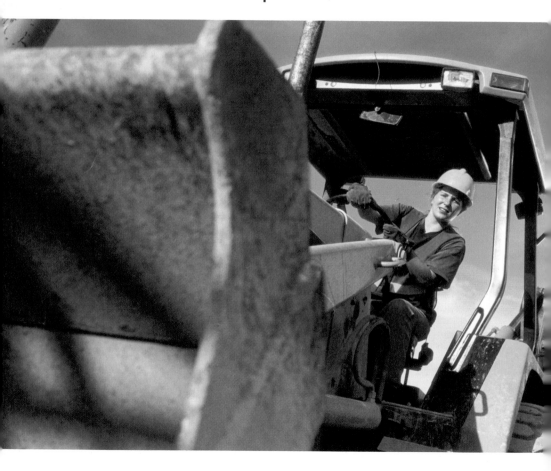

An **engine** gives an earthmover power.

The engine makes an earthmover's
tracks go around. Tracks keep an
earthmover from sinking in soft dirt.

Some earthmovers have rubber tires, not tracks. But tires can sink in soft dirt. They work best on hard dirt and roads.

An earthmover's engine makes its **arm** go up and down, too. What is at the end of this earthmover's arm?

A **bucket** is at the end of the arm.
Front-end loaders have wide buckets.
They are good for scooping earth.

Skid-steer loaders have buckets
with flat bottoms. They can scoop
or push earth.

Excavators have big buckets called
hoes. They can dig and dump piles
of dirt.

Backhoes have two buckets. The wide one in front is good for scooping.

The bucket in back is a hoe. That is why these earthmovers are called backhoes.

Some earthmovers have flat **blades**
instead of buckets. Bulldozers have
blades. They push big piles of earth.

Graders have blades, too. The blade is behind the front tires. It makes the earth smooth, like frosting on a cake.

Each earthmover has a job to do.
Look at the bucket. Look at the tracks.
Can you guess what job this earthmover
is doing?

This excavator is digging a hole for a new building. The operator dumps earth in a truck. The truck driver takes it away.

This earthmover has a funny shape.
What job is it doing?

This scraper is working on a new road. A wide pan hangs down in the middle of the scraper. Dirt slides into the pan as the scraper rolls along.

After the scraper, along comes a grader. Graders roll quickly on rubber tires. They make the dirt smooth and flat.

Next come rollers to pack the dirt. This
sheepsfoot roller has bumps. The
bumps leave a pattern in the dirt.

Earthmovers move earth. They dig in the dirt all day.

The earthmovers' work is done for today.

Facts about Earthmovers

■ Excavators have different nicknames
  in different parts of the United States.
  In some places, they are called shovels.
  In other places, they are called hoes.

■ When is a bobcat not a real cat?
  When it's a skid-steer loader.
  Skid-steer loaders are often called
  bobcats. A company called Bobcat
  makes many skid-steer loaders.

■ A large excavator can fill a whole
  dump truck with dirt from just two
  scoops of its bucket.

■ The sheepsfoot roller got its name
  from the prints it makes in the earth.
  It makes the ground look like hundreds
  of sheep walked over it.

Parts of a Backhoe

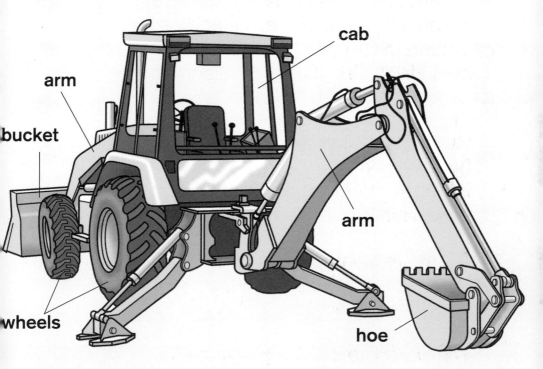

This backhoe is shown from the back. The operator's chair turns around so that the operator can move the bucket or the hoe.

Glossary

arm: the part of an earthmover that connects the main part to another part that digs or scoops

blade: the wide, flat part of a bulldozer or grader that pushes or smooths earth

bucket: the part of an earthmover that scoops and digs earth

engine: the part of an earthmover that gives it power and makes its parts move

hoe: a special kind of bucket on an excavator or a backhoe that digs earth

operator: the person who makes an earthmover work

tracks: wide belts that carry earthmovers over soft dirt

Index

About the Author

Susan Rand

Lee Sullivan Hill grew up in Massachusetts, where she loved to dig in the dirt. But her mother didn't appreciate the missing spoons! When she grew up, she worked in construction and watched earthmovers do the digging. Lee lives in Illinois with her husband, two sons, and two cats. This is her 20th book for children.

Photo Acknowledgments

The photographs in this book appear courtesy of: © Howard Ande, pp. 3, 4, 22, 23, 25; © Betty Crowell, pp. 5, 11; © Geostock/Photodisc, p. 6; © Todd Strand/Independent Picture Service, pp. 7, 9, 14, 20, 21, 26, 31; © Zigy Kaluzny/Stone, p. 8; © Hisham F. Ibrahim/Photodisc, p. 10; © Skip Nall/Photodisc, pp. 12, 13; © John Deere, pp. 15, 16, 17, 24; © PhotoLink/Photodisc, p. 18; © Patrick Clark/Photodisc, pp. 19, 27. Illustration on p. 29 by Laura Westlund, © Lerner Publications Company. Front cover: © John Deere. Back cover: © Todd Strand/Independent Picture Service.